Anger Managem

Mindful Guide to Manage Anger, Stress, and Emotions for a Peaceful and Happy Life.

By

Aiden Moseley

Deluxe Reads

About the Author

Aiden Moseley is a social activist and behavior specialist. He is a professional therapist and mainly focuses his energy on creating techniques and therapies that could help people of all ages. Aiden Moseley believes in creating a healthy environment that could be beneficial for everyone. He is currently working in an NGO that deals in providing mental and emotional therapies for kids and adults both. The different books he has written provides guidelines and effective therapies for its readers and he ensures they get the solution to their problem through the information they provide.

Table of contents

ABOUT THE AUTHOR...3

INTRODUCTION...5

CHAPTER 1: EMOTIONS, ANGER, AND STRESS 7

CHAPTER 2: MASTER YOUR EMOTIONS..14

2.1 Factors that Affect Emotions 15

2.2 How to Become the Boss of Your Emotions?..19

CHAPTER 3: HOW TO CONTROL YOUR ANGER BEFORE IT CONTROLS YOU..32

3.1 Triggers of Your Anger 32

3.2 Types and Causes of Anger..34

3.3 Effects of Anger Issues..38

3.4 How to Control Anger Issues? 40

CHAPTER 4: MANAGE YOUR STRESS 50

4.1 Triggers of Stress..51

4.2 Effects on Your Life..60

4.3 How to Manage Your Stress? 65

CONCLUSION 73

Introduction

The thoughts may create a heaven of Hell and a hell of Heaven. — JOHN MILTON, POET.

Thoughts come in awareness and then vanish as quickly as they appeared. Associating with your thoughts is deceptive, although some of them are useless. For example, the mental conversation that runs through your head when you see someone interacting with their kitten in the park. Although your neurological system records what you see, your mind feels obligated to add a discourse about what it sees. "What a cute kitten." Observing the kitten isn't enough; the mind is obliged to tell you the narrative of what it sees.

Therein lays the issue. The mind gives everyday occurrences that we accept new meaning. This narrative is frequently pessimistic. People prefer to focus on the bad rather than the good. As a result, the mind gets fixated on negative things, such as judgments, guilt, worry brought on by future ideas, etc.

Every person has negative thoughts throughout the day. The way we cope with these negative ideas, on the other hand, determines our life. It is totally up to you whether you want to ignore or embrace them. If you don't take steps to avoid pessimistic and unwelcoming ideas, they have the potential to manipulate you negatively and even suffocate your life and happiness. Because we are human, we may experience many unpleasant ideas during the day. However, it is important to consider how to prevent them as much as possible.

In the first chapter of this book, you will read the basics about emotions, anger, and stress and how they impact your peaceful life. The second chapter is about how to cope with your emotions. In the third chapter of this book, you will read about the triggers of your anger, how it can affect you, and how you can control your anger before it controls you. The fourth chapter of this book is about the basics of stress and practical solutions to cope with your stress.

This book will help its readers to maintain their positive emotions and minimize their negative emotions. It will also help its readers to manage their outbursts of negative emotions such as anger and stress.

Chapter 1: Emotions, Anger, and Stress

We all experience different kinds of emotions from a very young age. These emotions could be positive or negative. We rarely pay attention to these emotions. We do not consider the impact of this emotion on our minds and life. We also do not consider the long-term implication of holding on to such emotions. In this introductory chapter, we will deep dive into negative emotions such as anger and stress.

Emotions

- How are you doing today?
- Are you in a good or a bad mood?

When these questions are asked, it is quite likely that we can all determine which emotional state we are in at any specific time.

Emotions may have a great influence on your life and actions. Your everyday feelings may push you to act and influence the major and little judgments you take in your life. Emotions are affected by the central nervous system. Important components in our brain influence emotions and behavioral reactions.

It is very important to comprehend the three key aspects of emotion to comprehend it properly. Each part may influence the goal of your emotional experiences.

- Interpretive component: How you feel about it.

- Physiological component: Your body's reaction to your moods and feelings.
- The expressive component: How you react to the feeling.

There are many purposes for our emotions. Emotions may be brief, long-lasting, intense, complicated, and even life-altering. They can inspire us to act in certain ways and provide us with the abilities we need to engage effectively in our social lives.

- **Emotions Can Aid in Decision-Making**

Your emotional responses have a substantial impact on the choices you undertake, from where you go to who you like. Emotional intelligence, the capacity to recognize and control emotions, has been linked to better decision-making.

- **Emotions Assist Others in Understanding You**

It is vital to leave signs that help people understand how you are feeling while dealing with them. Emotional expressions in the form of body position, such as various emotions relating to the feelings you are undergoing, are examples of these signals. It may also require stating your thoughts directly while telling family or friends that you are glad, sad, excited, or afraid in various situations. You are giving them the knowledge that they can utilize right away to take action.

- **Emotions Assist You in Comprehending Others**

If you are connected with someone through social communication, you are providing them your information through your emotions and vice versa. Social communication is an important part of your daily life and family, and being capable of reading and responding to other people's emotions is essential.

It allows you to react appropriately and build more profound ties with friends, family, and dear ones. It also allows you to communicate effectively in a variety of social situations, such as coping with a cranky customer. Knowing how others communicate their emotions might help us determine how we should respond in a given situation.

- **Effects of Negative Emotions on Your Health**

People with good emotional health are conscious of their feelings, ideas, and actions. They know how to deal with the stress and other issues that come with life. They have positive self-esteem and healthy relationships with others.

However, many events in your life can wreak havoc on your mental well-being. These things can make you feel depressed, stressed, or anxious. Those that are pleasant or desired may be just as stressful as undesirable changes. Such as:

- Dealing with a loved one's death.
- Being afflicted with a disease or harm.
- Having financial difficulties.

The way you perceive, feel, and act affects your body. When you are stressed, nervous, or unhappy, your body signals that something is not quite right.

Anger

- Do you get annoyed quickly?

- Could you not control your fury when facing injustice?

- Could you feel your blood start to boil when someone degrades you?

All the feelings stated above are indications that you are getting angry. It is fine to be angry. Anger is a powerful emotion that can range from mild irritation to outright rage. Although many people think of rage as just a "bad mood," it may also be beneficial. Anger, if left unchecked, can lead to aggressive behavior, such as yelling at someone or smashing windows. Angry feelings may cause you to withdraw from society and concentrate your rage within, which can be harmful to both your physical and mental health.

Being able to control your anger does not mean you will never be angry. Rather, it requires learning to understand, moderate, and express outrage in a healthy and productive manner. Anger management is a skill that can be learned by everyone. Even if you think you've got your emotions under control, there's always room for improvement.

Anger may help us get through some difficult feelings and situations and inspire us to alter things in our lives that we do not like. It can become a problem when anger impacts a person's everyday life and/or relationships. Anger issues might indicate melancholy, despair, solitude, prejudice, or perhaps another psychological disorder.

Learning to recognize and express our anger safely and soundly is vital to maintaining good mental health. You can do several things to control your anger healthily if you are frequently angry or have difficulty regulating or expressing it.

What Makes You Angry?

The environment is a major contributor to a person's anger. It can be triggered by many factors, including stress, financial problems, violence, poor social or personal conditions, and burdensome demands on your time and energy. Your body's capacity to deal with various neurochemicals and your genetics have a part in how you cope with rage.

Impact on Our Peaceful Life

Anger can directly affect your peaceful life. It can affect your mental health, but it can also affect you physically.

Anger's Physical Repercussions

Anger activates the 'fight or flight reaction in the body. Panic, enthusiasm, and nervousness are other feelings that can cause this reaction. In anticipation of physical effort, the brain diverts blood away from the intestines and into the limbs. The temperature of the body rises, and the skin sweats profusely when the heart rate, blood pressure, and breathing increase.

The persistent rush of stress hormones and related metabolic changes that come with unchecked anger can eventually impair various physiological systems.

Unmanaged anger has been related to a variety of health issues, including:

- Headaches
- Digestive issues
- Sleeplessness increases anxiety
- Sadness
- Hypertension
- Stroke

Stress

Your body's response to tension from a circumstance or occurrence is called stress. It might be a psychological, intellectual, or bodily response. It is a common powerful emotion that everybody experiences at some time in their life. The human species, in fact, is designed to sense and react to stress. Your body creates physical and mental responses in reaction to the events or obstacles.

The stressful situations in your body help you adjust to new situations. Stress has the potential to be useful since it keeps us alert, focused, and ready to flee danger. If you have a rigorous challenge forthcoming, for instance, a stress response may prevent diseases and cause you to work harder and stay awake longer. It becomes an issue when tension persists without any periods of rest.

Impact of Stress on Your Peaceful Life

The nervous system controls your heart rate, respiration, eyesight, and other bodily functions. Physiological, intellectual, and behavioral expressions are all examples of indicators.

- Chest discomfort or a rushing feeling in your heart
- Tiredness or inability to sleep
- Headaches, vertigo, or tremors
- Hypertension
- Clenching of the jaw
- Digestive or stomach issues
- Immune system deficiency
- Anxiety or irritation are two emotional and mental symptoms that might arise due to stress.

In the next chapters, you will deeply learn how to cope with emotions, anger, and stress. I also have mentioned the practical methods to manage emotions, anger, and stress.

Chapter 2: Master Your Emotions

The value of your life is determined by how you feel. Your emotions have the power to make or break your life. That is why they are one of the most crucial things you have to pay attention to.

All of your encounters are colored by your emotions. It all seems or feels good when you are in a good mood. You also think more clearly. Your enthusiasm level increases and the options appear to be endless. When you are sad, everything appears dull. You are tired and discouraged due to a lack of energy. You are stuck in a spot you would rather not be, and a bleak outlook appears.

Emotions can also serve as strong guidance. They can alert you to a problem and help you make adjustments in your life. As a result, they might be one of your most effective personal development tools. Unfortunately, neither schools nor parents educate kids on how to understand or regulate their emotions. Have you ever been given a guidebook that explains how your brain operates and how to utilize it to regulate your emotions better? I have not done so.

In this chapter, you will discover how to master your feelings or keep them under control. Let's get this started.

2.1 Factors that Affect Emotions

Emotions are complicated, and a multitude of variables influences them. We will go through some of the factors that influence your emotions. The best part is that you can also influence them.

Most of your feelings are self-made if we remove impulsive, emotional reactions. They are the product of how you perceive ideas and situations. However, these are not the only factors that influence your mental state. Your physique, tone, the cuisine you take, and how much sleep you get all contribute to the effectiveness of your emotions and, as a result, affect your life. Let's look at how each of these factors affects your emotions.

- **You Become What You Think**

Every day, we have somewhere between 9000 to 70,000 thoughts. This thinking can lead to mental, emotional, and physical problems. Therefore, understanding how ideas operate and how thoughts affect our health and well-being is essential. Your ideas cause you to feel, and you act on that emotion. And that action defines your choices and life.

Emotions and thoughts have a significant impact on each another. Worrying about an upcoming job interview might generate anxiety, and thoughts can also act as an assessment of that emotion. Furthermore, how we pay attention to and evaluate our experiences impacts our well-being. A person who has a phobia of dogs, for example, is likely hyperaware of the dog all over the street and perceives the dog's presence as menacing, resulting in emotional discomfort. A person who considers the dog's presence pleasant will have a different emotional reaction to the same event.

- **Your Sleeping Schedule and Your Emotions**

✓ Do you have a habit of forgetting stuff?
✓ Is it difficult for you to focus on challenging opportunities?
✓ Do you sleep for fewer than six hours per night?

If this is the case, you are most likely not sleeping properly. A lack of sleep may also make it difficult to think effectively and regulate your emotions. Consider how you experience the next day after a terrible night's sleep or not getting enough sleep. Many of us are irritated and angry, struggle to focus, and have little energy. When situations do not go our way, we tend to overreact, and when things go well, we tend to be less enthusiastic. It's easy to understand how chronic insomnia may affect our emotions. Long-term sleep deprivation raises the danger of chronic illnesses, including heart problems. It can also have a big impact on your mood.

Sleep deprivation and emotional problems are intimately related, and both of them can impact your emotions: sleep deprivation may affect your emotions, and emotions can influence how much and how well you sleep. Sleep deprivation has been linked to increased negative thoughts. Sleep deprivation is a common sign of mood disorders, including sadness and anxiety. It can even lead to some mental disorders.

Your mood might have an impact on how well you sleep. Anxiety and stress cause restlessness and keep your body awake, attentive, and stimulated. You could notice that you can't put your thoughts off, your heart is racing, and your respiration is short and rapid. As a result, obtaining enough sleep and the correct sleep is critical.

✓ **Environment and Your Emotions**

Humans have been required to be responsive to their surroundings from the beginning of time, which means we have an intrinsic understanding of our surroundings and search out situations with certain features.

First and foremost, people need safety and support, and they seek such qualities in their surroundings. Furthermore, we desire a psychologically pleasant setting, such as one that is familiar yet provides just the appropriate amount of stimulation.

People's interactions can be aided or hindered by their surroundings. Their surroundings can influence people's conduct and drive them to act. A filthy corridor full of additional hospital equipment, for example, will encourage staff to leave another item in the hall. Still, a clean corridor with abundant storage will urge staff to remove the item. The surroundings do have an impact on one's mood. In short, our surroundings can create or relieve stress, which has various effects on our bodies.

✓ Social Culture and Your Emotions

Culture, values, behavior, and material goods that make up a person's way of life, may influence how they express, perceive, and feel emotions. Culture provides rigidity, rules, perceptions, and regulations to interpret and perceive different feelings. Culture may also guide how people choose to manage their emotions, trying to influence an individual's emotional journey and leading to overall diverse cultures in the expertise and showcase of emotion. For example, communal peace is valued above individual gain in many Asian cultures, but Westerners in most of Europe value individual self-promotion.

Various cultures have different social implications for different emotions: in the United States, males are frequently directly or indirectly stigmatized for crying; among the Utku Eskimo society, expressing rage can lead to social ostracism.

Different rules may be internalized due to an individual's gender, class, family history, or another element within society. For example, there is some indication that men and women regulate their emotions differently, maybe due to culturally driven gender pressures and practices. Although cultural standards for expressing emotion differ, our capacity to perceive and make corresponding facial emotions seems fundamental.

2.2 How to Become the Boss of Your Emotions?

What if I assure you that by mastering just one technique, you could have rock-hard abs, extra money, and accomplish your goals? You would undoubtedly be curious as to what it is. I am going to tell you how to control your emotions on this topic. What steps you can take to have control over your emotions.

First, you must understand that managing your emotions does not imply becoming emotionless. To reach the desired objective, mastering your emotions allows you to boost or soothe your personal and others' emotions consciously. Let's get this started.

- **Own and Accept Your Emotions**

According to modern psychological studies, emotional avoidance is one of the major causes of many psychiatric issues. This may come as a surprise because avoiding bad feelings seems to be a sensible goal. Terrible emotions, after all, do not feel nice, and they are frequently associated in our thoughts with negative occurrences that we prefer to prevent or ignore. Furthermore, we are all aware of the temporary respite that avoidance may bring.

In the short term, avoidance is an efficient option. However, in the long term, it creates a greater issue than the one evaded in the first instance. The short-term benefit comes with long-term misery when you avoid unpleasant feelings.

For example: When you drink to prevent the brief unpleasantness of a bad mood, you are similar to someone who drinks when they are stressed. When the terrible sensations return the next day, he drinks again. It could be good for a short-term period. However, in the long term, that individual would acquire a more serious problem (addiction) than the unsolved concerns he ignored by drinking.

- **Emotional Avoidance is Damaging**

Life ambitions may include passing through difficult times and places, but if you refuse to face the difficulties of your journey, it may unnecessarily limit your life horizons. Evasion becomes a cage over time because you tend to feel such a need to flee numerous circumstances, people, experiences, and locations that may bring up, stir up, or remind you of the negative emotion. Attempting to prevent unpleasant feelings almost always fails. Therefore, emotional avoidance frequently entails the denial of reality, which is not a solid basis for healthy existence.

As a person, you will experience a wide range of emotions, just as there are many different types of weather. These feelings are, above all else, a natural component of being a human being. You are expressing your complete humanity by recognizing your emotional existence.

Accepting and experiencing unpleasant emotions and acknowledging and absorbing them is referred to as emotional acceptance. Acceptance has several advantages. To begin with, embracing your feelings is accepting the reality of your life and situation. This acceptance eliminates the need to use energy to drive the emotion away. Instead, once you have acknowledged the feeling, you may focus on engaging in activities in line with your aims and beliefs.

By accepting your feelings, you give yourself the incentive to understand them, grow acquainted with them, develop skills in their control, and incorporate them into your existence. Therefore, avoidance won't teach you that. You have to remind yourself of this fact every time when you are feeling negative emotions. "Negative feelings maybe hurtful, but they will not kill you."

Finally, when you embrace unpleasant feelings, their destructive force diminishes. Many people find this strange, but if you consider it for a moment, you will understand its logic. When trapped in an undertow in a sea, swimmers typically panic and start swimming against the current with all their strength. They frequently become exhausted, cramp, and drown. To live, such a swimmer must do the opposite: let go. Allow the tide to carry him out to sea. The current will diminish after a few hundred yards, allowing the swimmer to swim around again and back to shore. It is the same with strong emotion. Fighting it is pointless and sometimes hazardous.

- **Label Your Emotions**

✓ What are your current feelings?
✓ Which emotions have you experienced today?

Most of you would likely reply "good" or "not good" to the first question. When you came to the second question, you generally came up with a tiny number of feelings, anywhere between two and five emotions. I know it because there is substantial evidence that it is difficult to accurately recognize and classify the wide range of emotions we encounter daily. Importantly, some people have a harder time naming their feelings than others. They come up with a few categories to explain their feelings, no matter how complicated they are. To put it another way, the less conscious we are of our feelings, the more difficult it is to figure out how to manage them effectively. Putting bad emotions into words might help you manage them.

There are three methods to utilize labeling to calm yourself down if you are experiencing a strong emotion:

1. Consider it

Have a brief, silent dialogue with yourself. It may go like this, "What emotion am I experiencing right now?"

2. Write about it

Not only can people who write about deeply emotional experiences enhance their health in quantifiable measurements, but writing can also help you perform better in emotional circumstances.

3. Declare it

Admit the emotion that you have written. You need to name your emotional state, but do not use it as a weapon. Just say it plainly, like this, "I'm becoming a little agitated right now."

As a result, recognizing and naming emotions allows us to take a step back and decide what to do with them. Emotions are just a sort of energy that is always looking for a way to express itself. Surprisingly, expressing how we are feeling might help us better regulate and control even the most unpleasant emotions.

- **Self-Care**

It is the process of taking care of oneself. It refers to a conscious action taken by a person to improve their physical, mental, and sentimental well-being. Self-care can take many different forms. It could be getting enough sleep each night or getting some fresh air by having to step outside for a few minutes. It is necessary to build courage in the midst of life's unavoidable unpleasant emotions. Once you've made significant improvements in taking control of the mind and body, you'll be in the greatest position to live your finest possible life.

Many individuals, sadly, see self-care as a privilege instead of a need. As a consequence, they feel burdened, fatigued, and unprepared to face life's unavoidable problems. Trying to find ways to relax is not the only aspect of self-care. It is about looking after your mental, physical, emotional, social, and spiritual well-being. It is critical to find the right balance that enables you to confront each of these areas to care for your wellness and well-being.

Caring About Your Body

You should take care of yourself if you need your body to perform correctly. It is essential to know that your mental and physical health are closely intertwined. If you maintain your body, you will feel about things better.

Physical self-care includes nourishing your body, how much regular exercise you get, and how good you look after your physical requirements. Physical self-care includes going to doctor's visits, taking medicine as recommended, and keeping track of your health. When it comes to actual self-care, consider the following questions to see if there are any areas where you can improve:

✓ Are you getting enough rest?
✓ Is your diet properly nourishing your body?
✓ Do you have control over your health?
✓ Do you receive enough physical activity?

Self-Care for the Mind

The way you think and the ideas that engage your thoughts to have a big impact on your emotional health. Inner self-care also includes things that help you remain mentally healthy. Conscience and tolerance, for example, may aid in the development of a more pleasant inner narrative. When thinking about your mental self-care, consider the following questions:

- ✓ Do you devote enough time to cognitively stimulating activities?
- ✓ Are you taking proactive steps to maintain your mental health?

Self-Care for Emotions

Make yourself a priority. It includes your mental health as well. Activities that help you recognize and share your emotions regularly and safely may be included in emotional self-care. It is critical to include empathy and selflessness into your life, whether you chat to a spouse or close friend about how you are feeling or set aside time for relaxation that helps you manage your feelings. Consider the following questions while evaluating your emotional self-care strategies:

- ✓ Do you have a healthy way of dealing with your emotions?
- ✓ Do you include things in your daily routine that make you feel re-energized?

Creating a Self-Care Strategy

A good self-care strategy should be personalized to your lifestyle and requirements. It must be something you have made yourself, for yourself. Creating your self-care strategy might serve as a preventative tool to keep you from being overwhelmed, overstressed, or burned out. The following stages can assist you in developing your self-care plan:

- ✓ **Determine your requirements:** Make a list of the many aspects of life and the primary activities you participate in daily. You could mention work, school, friendships, and family.
- ✓ **Think about your stressors:** Consider the parts of these regions that give you tension and how you could deal with that stress.
- ✓ **Come up with self-care strategies:** Consider some things that you may engage in to reduce stress and anxiety. Building good social ties may be as simple as hanging out with friends or learning to set limits.
- ✓ **Prepare for challenges:** If you see that you are ignoring a certain element of your life, make a strategy to change it.
- ✓ **Start small:** You do not have to take on everything simultaneously. Determine one modest move you can do to improve your self-care.

You will discover that when you take care of yourself, you will be able to work more successfully and quickly.

- • **Stop Suppressing and Start Reappraising**

When it comes to dealing with uncomfortable emotions, most individuals respond in one of the two ways: they act out or suppress them. When you behave out of a powerful feeling like rage, you will almost certainly negatively affect your relationships and your surroundings. The dangers of repressing those powerful emotions are considerably worse.

Many people are unaware that there is another method to control our emotions, that is, experiencing them in real-time. Emotions are, on one level, like energy waves that change in shape and strength, much like ocean waves. Their nature, like all-natural events, is for them to appear and vanish swiftly. Several things can happen if you stop this process by acting out or repressing it.

You must reappraise them. If you want to let go of those emotions, you should own them properly and feel them. If you do not express your feelings, you will suffer psychologically and physically. Repressing your emotions, anger, sorrow, grief, or irritation can cause physical tension. Even though the basic feeling is different, the result is the same.

- **Keep a Mood Journal**

  ✓ Have you ever noticed how you make poor decisions when you are furious?
  ✓ You can't think straight when you are depressed.

It is not unexpected that our mood significantly impacts how we think and make decisions. It is for this reason that we must keep track of it. This is not the same as keeping a diary of your everyday activities. Rather, it is a method of recognizing and acting on your emotions. It has been proven that journaling your ideas, emotions, and issues can help you feel less anxious. A mood diary will help you better understand how to enhance your mental health.

How to Keep a Journal of Your Mood?

While prefabricated emotion diaries are purchasable, no specific equipment or supplies are required to get started. A blank notepad and a pen are all you need. Outline the following columns before night, or anytime you have a few small moments, to help you think on a few of your most important feelings from the day:

- ✓ Name of an emotion
- ✓ What triggered that feeling?
- ✓ You have adopted the following behaviors or taken the following activities due to this mood.
- ✓ Is this feeling suitable for the circumstances?
- ✓ Is this a situation that must be endured or one that must be resolved?

Keeping track of your emotions can help you develop your mental health. They will eventually rule you if you do not learn to manage your emotions, which is a formula for catastrophe. Here are some reasons why I think you should start keeping a mood diary.

1. It Assists You in Deciding on a Course of Action

You can better grasp what you need if you are conscious of your feelings. Consider the last time you felt yourself emotionally whirling. Did you feel like you were in a position to choose? Most likely not.

When you are overwhelmed, it is difficult to take action. A mood notebook can assist you in noticing your daily feelings so that you may choose the best methods to respond to them.

2. It Aids in the Expression of Emotions

If you are prone to thinking and fretting about everything, writing is an excellent way to express yourself. A mood diary is a secure environment where you may express yourself without fear of being judged. It's a process that's both healing and liberating. Because you're conversing with yourself, you don't have to be concerned about how others will receive your remarks.

3. It will Assist You in Your Recovery

Keeping a journal has always been an important part of my recovery process whenever I have had a major trauma in my life. I have only felt worse when I have attempted to put down or ignore uncomfortable feelings from my past.

Mood journaling assists you in sorting through the tough events in your life so that you can begin to make sense of them. More significantly, this therapy process helps you better understand yourself, which is essential for healing. It is your birthright to be healed. I advise you to start writing your way to improved mental and emotional health if you have been battling to construct meaning of the trauma you have experienced.

4. It Aids in the Discovery of Your Triggers

Emotional triggers exist in all of us. It is a component of what it is to be human. These triggers could be anyone and anything, and they can cause you to lose your cool and disturb your mental health. Emotional triggers may be individuals, phrases, attitudes, events, or environmental factors that cause us to have a strong and uncontrollable emotional reaction.

- **Deep Breath Practicing**

Take a minute and breathe deeply in and exhale slowly. Let it out now. You may have already noticed a difference in your mood.

Your breath is a key factor in reducing anxiety and decreasing stress. If you incorporate some easy breathing exercises into your daily practice, they can significantly impact you. Deep breathing does not have to consume a lot of your time. It is just a matter of scheduling some time to focus on your breathing. Here is a simple method for you to get started:

- ✓ Use a mental image and a set of words to assist you in feeling relaxed while doing deep breathing.
- ✓ If your eyes are open, close them.
- ✓ Take a few deep breaths and exhale slowly.

- ✓ Inhale deeply. Assume that the air is overwhelmed with a notion of peace and tranquility as you do so. Try to sense it all over your body.
- ✓ Take a deep breath out. Imagine the air leaving with your stress and tension while doing it.
- ✓ Now, with your breath, say a word or phrase. "I breathe in peace and calm," repeat in your mind as you inhale. "I breathe out stress and tension," repeat in your mind as you exhale.
- ✓ Keep going for another 10 to 20 minutes.

Chapter 3: How to Control Your Anger Before It Controls You

Everyone gets irritated from time to time. It will become a problem when anger starts to affect a person's everyday life and drives them to respond in ways that may harm them or others.

Anger is a strong emotion that ranges from slight discomfort to outright fury and rage. When you feel furious, your breathing and heart rate rise. Externally and internally, events can both trigger anger. You could feel furious at a particular person or incident or be upset because you are worried or brooding over personal issues. Memories of painful or upsetting situations can also trigger anger.

3.1 Triggers of Your Anger

Anger triggers are similar to any other type of emotional trigger. Emotional triggers exist in all of us. Various situations might elicit complicated emotions for everyone. So, have you ever noticed your triggers?

The distinction is in your real-life experiences. Your brain is trained to behave in various ways due to the things you encounter in life. The list of such triggers is practically unlimited. It might be a specific word, an act, a location, or a person; the list is endless. It is whatever your brain identifies with a specific memory from your life.

Understanding Your Anger Triggers

Triggers are not easy to understand since you might not be conscious of them. Most people say that "I just lose all control of my emotions, but I don't understand why." Your emotions are stimulated without your knowledge in these many circumstances.

To know an anger trigger, you must first determine what is causing you to become enraged. Through anger management treatment, you will know how to recognize and be more conscious of your anger triggers.

The cornerstone for excellent therapy is knowledge of your triggers. One of the most rewarding aspects of therapy is pushing stuff to your attention so you may change how they affect your life. Being conscious of your anger triggers allows you to take charge of your emotions. You can start to change it if you know what's causing your rage. Anger triggers are frequently the outcome of mental distress. The trigger will determine the amount of work you will have to accomplish.

Your wife, for instance, might be the source of your rage. You will probably need to think about how hate harms your relationship in this scenario. To adjust your anger trigger in this circumstance, you will need to focus on forgiving.

Anger triggers frequently necessitate working through hurtful or stressful events in your life. Things like being subjected to abuse, being assaulted by someone, or being in a scenario where your protection was in jeopardy are all common traumatic events linked to rage.

3.2 Types and Causes of Anger

Anger is an emotion that everyone experiences at some point in their lives. We are all angry, irritated, or offended from time to time. However, there is a prevalent misperception regarding anger: it always displays itself in the form of yelling or physical behavior. Anger is far subtler and more sophisticated than that. To control your anger, you must first identify the anger you are experiencing. The most typical forms of rage are listed below. If you can recognize the methods of your anger, you will be able to better manage it.

- **Indirect Rage**

Rage that does not manifest itself as anger is passive or indirect anger. Instead, anger manifests itself in little ways, such as snarky remarks or acts of unacknowledged hostility directed towards the individual you are angry at.

Internally, passive rage might be addressed. This is particularly true if you have suppressed your anger to the point that you do not even realize you are upset. Stress eating, panic episodes, excessive drinking or buying, unpredictable behavior, or self-harming are possibilities.

- **Explosive Anger**

This rage is different from passive anger. You and everybody

else know you are furious when you are in
fury. This type of rage is frequently violer.
uncontrollable. It is easy to lose control, resulting in w.
and acts that you will quickly regret after it passes.

Rejection and suppression are frequently at the root of
explosive rage, just as with indirect anger. This rage screams
out loud and clear rather than oozing out in little, often
unnoticeable ways.

- **Fear-Based Anger**

It can sometimes be easier to be angry than it is to be fear. This
is particularly true if we are concerned about the safety of
someone we care about. And besides, no one is more capable
of harming us than those closest to us. As a result, we may
respond with wrath when we observe them acting in ways
that might hurt them in a certain way.

This type of anger has effects in the short term. We may direct
our rage at a loved one, deliberately or subconsciously, to
startle them out of the behaviors that fear us.
Displaying rage when what we are truly experiencing is fear.
It may cause hurt, anxiety, and anger in the people we care
about.

- **Anger Caused by Frustration**

Distress rage is similar to fear-based anger when aimed
against a loved one. We do have the utmost standards and
aspirations for individuals we care about. We become irritated

whenever we see them fall short of what we believe is their best ability, and this disappointment all too frequently turns into anger.

Frustration-based rage can also be focused inside. Perhaps we are dissatisfied with life. Perhaps we believe that others have what we lack. We observe as everyone else seems to flourish and succeed, while we find it difficult to get through one setback after another. This type of rage stems from comparing how life is to some lofty ideal of how life should be. However, reality will never match the fantasy, whether your idea is for yourself or your loved ones.

- **Fury based on Suffering**

This is a sort of anger that frequently conceals hurt, anguish, or even severe depression. Pain and melancholy are two of the tough emotions to deal with. Anger is easier for some individuals since it may make you feel powerful, even if only for a while, but melancholy and despair can make you feel weak.

When despair threatens to consume you, rage might feel like the only tool you have to fight back. In reality, it aggravates the situation. This form of fury fails to treat the underlying suffering and adds to it—the anguish of regret, loneliness, and guilt.

- **Manipulative Rage**

Manipulative rage resembles chronic anger in many ways. It is utilized to exert influence over others, whether consciously or unconsciously. It is frequently loud. The idea is to make others around you comply by shocking them. Of course, such attempts to control will backfire long since your targets will only put up with so much commotion before walking out the door.

- **Overwhelmed Anger**

There is no denying that life is difficult. You usually feel like you are barely keeping your head above water some days. We are especially prone to "overwhelmed fury" at this time. This is the type of rage that occurs when life becomes too much. It is frequently the result of neglecting to take care of oneself, such as not getting enough sleep, eating nutritiously, exercising, or de-stressing.

- **Righteous Rage**

This is the type of anger that may be used for good. This is a form of rage with a purpose. The type of rage motivates you to take action—righting a wrong, defending the weak and innocent. This is the type of rage that helps to improve the world.

Causes of Anger

After you have determined your anger type, you will need to figure out what is causing your problem. So that you can control it using the proper technique. Both intrinsic and extrinsic factors can trigger anger. A person or an event can trigger anger. You can be enraged because someone next to you in line cut in front of you. You may get enraged when you are emotionally upset, frightened, in pain, or in a conflict.

Anger can mask other feelings we do not want to deal with, such as emotional anguish, fear, isolation, or loss. Anger becomes a personal trait in these situations. Anger can be a reaction to severe discomfort, fear, or to defend oneself from a projected assault. It can also be a response to stressful circumstances. Anger is caused by many factors that might be reasonable or irrational. These factors can be, including:

- ✓ Coping with a loved one's death
- ✓ Loss of employment
- ✓ Experiencing a breakup
- ✓ Losing at a job or completing a task
- ✓ Feeling tired

3.3 Effects of Anger Issues

Anger may seriously hurt you, your relationship with others, and your physical and emotional health.

- **Physical Consequences**

When you get angry, your heart is put in jeopardy. Anger's influence on your heart health is the most physically harmful. The risk of a heart attack doubles in the three hours after an angry rant. Heart disease is linked to repressed anger when you show it discreetly or take tremendous measures to restrain it.

Anger increases your chances of having a stroke. Be cautious if you tend to lash out. During the two hours following an emotional tirade, there was a threefold increased chance of suffering a stroke due to a blood clot in the brain. Patients with an abnormality in one of the brain's arteries following an emotional outburst had a six-fold increased chance of the artery perforating. It also causes your immune response to deteriorate. If you are always angry, you can become ill more frequently. Your lungs can be harmed by anger. If you are a permanently angry, aggressive person, you might still be harming your lungs.

- **Problems with Mental Health**

What about the psychological and emotional consequences of rage? Sure, none of us enjoys writhing in rage or lashing out at our family members, but we do not grasp the psychological consequences. It puts you in a bad mood, escalating to sadness, self-doubt, and loneliness. As you grumble in your rage, you may drive others away, including those who love you the most, only aggravating your mood.

- **Problems with Relationships**

Anyone who has ever been in a relationship understands how difficult it can be. Every partnership is made up of flawed individuals who have varying expectations. And while many couples recognize that they will not always agree, they do not see the dangers of rage in their relationship.

Anger that is not managed appropriately in a relationship can cause detrimental effects. If you are frequently reacting in excessive fury to the scenario, you may cause problems in your relationship. Your spouse may opt to quit the relationship if they are tired of the turmoil.

It is also simple to become enraged when others are enraged with you. That means the assertion will continue to worsen until you yell at each other or take the opposite approach and choose to disregard each other entirely. When neither party can maintain their composure, a little quarrel might escalate into a major one. When rage is allowed to spiral out of control, it can lead to verbal, psychological, or physical violence. In a partnership, no type of abuse is acceptable. This might include calling the other individuals names, demeaning them, or physically striking or injuring them.

3.4 How to Control Anger Issues?

Failure to control your anger may result in various issues, including regrettable statements, shouting at your children, and scaring coworkers. You have to balance your anger. However, regulating your emotions does not mean you will never again be angry. It involves learning to identify, regulate, and feel outraged in a healthy and productive manner. So, let's get started.

Recognizing the Warning Signs

You must first learn to spot your rage before learning how to regulate your emotions. You will need queries like:

- ✓ "What occurrences, individuals, situations, or things irritate me?"
- ✓ "When I am furious, how do I respond?"
- ✓ "How does my rage influence other people?"

It takes a long time to address these inquiries. It is possible that you can think of a few things that irritate you. You may be able to recognize a few indicators that you show when you are upset. You will need to keep asking yourself these inquiries for a while before you are confident that you completely understand your rage.

How can You Understand Your Anger Signals?

Learning to identify when you are furious is the first step toward successful emotional regulation. Some furious people regard their emotions as either black or white — they are either enraged or calm. Anger, in actuality, is not black and white but instead a complex grey area.

Individuals more susceptible to seeing anger in terms of extremes may struggle to recognize it while encountering moderate anger levels. Fortunately, most individuals are aware of various indicators that might alert them to the fact that they are getting disturbed. You may experience the following emotions:

- ✓ Irritated
- ✓ Depressed or unhappy

- ✓ Awful
- ✓ Resentful
- ✓ Worried
- ✓ A desire for a drink, a cigarette, or other relaxing things
- ✓ Starting to shout, yell, or cry

- **Workout When You Are Angry**

When anger becomes uncontrollable, it becomes a problem. Some people engage in physical activity to help them cope with their moods and concerns. Exercise has been shown to lower anxiety, sadness, and aggression. Some individuals may find it difficult to devote their effort to an exercise while they are angry.

When you are angry or frustrated, there are several approaches to movement. Some people vent their frustrations through explosive activities like boxing or interval training. Others may prefer mind-body exercises like yoga or Tai Chi.

It is also possible that what succeeds in one event is not as successful in another. So, keep an open mind and try various activities to help you relax. It is important to remember that the purpose of a workout is not always to get rid of anger. Anger is a normal emotion that may be beneficial. Exercise simply provides you with a means of expressing and managing your emotions healthily. The preceding exercises, in particular, assist you in focusing on various movement difficulties to momentarily divert your attention away from the point of your rage.

a. Boxing

Workouts in boxing need you to concentrate on certain punch and jab sequences. A boxing workout involves the entire body, boosts metabolism, and increases strength, particularly in the upper body. Boxing at home does not require a large financial investment. You may buy gloves and other punching equipment, then use a mobile application to train.

b. Rope Jumping

Jumping rope is another elevated activity that needs focus and attention. The benefit of this workout is that it swiftly raises your pulse rate and burns calories. It also necessitates the use of very minimal equipment.

c. Yoga

It has been proven that mind-body techniques can help decrease blood pressure. When you feel angry, you might want to try one of the many various forms of yoga available.

- ✓ Hatha yoga is a slower, gentler kind of yoga.
- ✓ Power yoga and rhythmic yoga move faster and provide a more rigorous exercise.
- ✓ Harbin yoga is done in a warm environment, which might make it difficult to concentrate on certain poses for the whole 90-minute session. There is a style of yoga specifically developed to help people vent their rage.

If you are performing yoga at home, all you need is a yoga mat and some space, irrespective of the practice you select. You can use a yoga app or take an online course.

d. Tai Chi

Tai chi is a sort of art form that emerged in China. It is a succession of flowing motions and self-meditation. If you find yourself fired up and agitated, the gradual rhythm of the exercise may help you calm down and lower your pulse rate. There are several styles of tai chi, but there are tai chi courses on the internet and smartphone applications that can assist you if you are just looking to start.

e. Meditation

While meditation is not an exercise, it is an inner activity that may help you understand to focus awareness and interest for clarity of mind. It has been proven that mindful meditation relieves stress and hostility. You do not need to take a class to meditate, although you might want to explore the internet, read some books, or utilize an app to get started.

f. Walking

Walking has several advantages, including improved cardiac health and a lower chance of chronic illnesses like type 2 diabetes. Jogging may also be a good method to let off steam. When you feel annoyed or exhausted, grab a companion and go for a stroll. Or you can go alone for a walk and appreciate the solitude.

g. Hiking

Walking on a hilly path, such as woods or steep ridges, is also a way to let go of tension and anger. Interaction with nature has been proved helpful in research to have a meaningful impact on your body.

- **Applying Management Techniques**

Anger outbursts may be dangerous to both you and others around you. Anger management exercises are a fantastic technique to cool down and prevent any loss. These methods operate by first calming you down and then assisting you in taking good steps forward. Any time you feel your anger is overpowering, do the accompanying anger management techniques until you feel calm.

Learn to Breathe Properly

You may notice that your breathing becomes faster and quicker when you are furious. Slowing and deepening your breathing is a simple method to relax your body and minimize irritation. Slowly inhale deeply and exhale through your mouth. Instead of breathing from your chest, take deep breaths from your abdomen. As needed, repeat the breaths.

Relax Your Muscles

When you are upset, you may experience muscle tightness, which indicates stress in the body. You might wish to attempt a gradual muscle relaxation method to help you relax. This entails tensing and then releasing each specific muscle in the body. Start from the top of your head and work your way down to your toes, or the other way around.

Visualize Yourself Being at Ease

Imagine a peaceful environment to help you calm down. Shut your eyes for a few seconds and sit in a peaceful, pleasant place from your recollection. Allow your imagination to go wild. Consider minor things as you imagine what that pleasant area is like. What does it smell like? What does it sound like? Consider how relaxed and at ease you are in that location.

Get Your Feet Moving

As you have read before, regular exercise is particularly helpful in decreasing muscular tension and mind and being beneficial for your biological systems. To prevent frustration and tension at bay:

- ✓ Try to get some workout every day.
- ✓ Take a vigorous walk, ride a bike, or run to relieve stress quickly.
- ✓ When you feel your wrath rising, go for a walk or engage in physical activity.

Recognize Your Triggers

Anger triggers have also been discussed before. You must know your triggers very well. Normally, people are prone to be enraged over the same things repeatedly. Things that may affect your mental health for a long time. If it is feasible for you, try to prevent or cope with their triggers.

For example: Instead of becoming furious over the clutter that your child has made, you may lock the door to your child's room when they do not clean it.

If you are easily irritated by traffic, you should avoid traffic by taking a route that has less traffic.

Take a Moment to Listen

When you are in a heated disagreement, it is easy to rush to judgment and say harsh words. Stopping and listening to the other people in the discussion before responding might help you control your emotions and respond and settle the matter more effectively. Before you respond, give it some thought. Tell them you have to backtrack if you need to calm off before continuing the talk.

Change the Way You Think

Anger might make you believe that things are much worse than they are. Replace negative ideas with much more reasonable ones to calm down. When you think, try to avoid using extreme terms like "never" or "always."

Refrain from Ruminating on the Same Topics

Even if the matter has been handled, you may remember the same circumstance that disturbed you. This is known as obsessing or dwelling. Dwelling encourages anger to aggravate, potentially leading to further disputes or other problems. You should move on from the source of your rage and focus on the good aspects of a person.

Seeking a Psychologist for Anger

If your anger cannot be managed by yourself or by following the above instructions, you need to consult a psychologist to manage your anger. Psychologist helps you in managing your anger by using different therapies.

The most common rage therapy has been cognitive-behavioral therapy (CBT). You learn to recognize and alter harmful or unpleasant thinking patterns with CBT. Stress Immunization is one CBT-based rage therapy. This strategy entails exposing you to fictitious circumstances that might cause you to get angry and chances to self-monitor your rage and practice coping techniques. Other strategies for managing anger have received less attention, although several seem to have merit. These are some of them:

Family therapy assists members of the same family resolve conflicts and communicating effectively. It might be beneficial in dealing with rage issues aimed at a loved partner or children.

Psychodynamic therapy is a type of treatment in which therapists assist clients in focusing on the psychological underpinnings of their emotional discomfort through self-reflection.

Anger is frequently associated with other issues such as post-traumatic stress disorder (PTSD), anxiety, and alcoholism. Psychologists can assist in the treatment of such disorders and the management of the anger that comes with those.

Chapter 4: Manage Your Stress

Stress is an inescapable part of life. It is more crucial than ever to recognize stress and how to deal with it. Because stress may not badly affect your mental health, but it may also give you headaches, upset stomach, chest pain, and the problem with sleep. While stress may be good, it can also be dangerous if prolonged. Once the body detects a crisis, it moves into constant alert mode, and it swiftly recovers after the threat has passed.

Health concerns, employment, income, family problems, discrimination or gender inequity, and everyday annoyances are all examples of stressors. Your body may be in a permanent condition of heightened alert due to relentless or too many stimuli, leading to poor focus, unpleasant emotions, job strain, and emotional health issues. When stress is prolonged, the body struggles to operate normally. Chronic stress has been related to cardiovascular disease, hypertension, diabetes, despair, and mood disorders.

Stress has varied effects on men and women. Women are more likely than males to suffer from stress-related illnesses such as depression and anxiousness. Personal differences exist in addition to sex and gender disparities. Some people have a higher level of resiliency than others. They are less or more affected by stress, and they may even do best under pressure. "There's an adage that goes, 'It is not how far you hit, but how much you rebound.' That's wonderful news for all of us who don't rebound back as quickly. To some extent, perseverance can be taught, and there are a few easy, realistic things most people can do to change things.

To understand how to manage your stress, you need to learn about your stress triggers. Let's get started.

4.1 Triggers of Stress

The doorbell rings, your children start bickering and yelling your nickname, and the pan of pasta you're preparing starts to boil over because you're preparing supper. Everybody else is vying for your focus, and you're already exhausted. These are instances of stressful events which last for a short period and can be helpful to your wellness. However, if your stressors are consistently high, you may be suffering from serious stress, a sort of long stress that is harmful for your health.

When you are overburdened with obligations that force you to respond or adapt, you experience stress. Finance, romantic relations, employment, education, or any other scenario that you consider to be challenging can all contribute to stress causes. Emotionally, intellectually, and socially, your body reacts to these difficulties.

Stress is an unavoidable aspect of life. It is, in fact, necessary for your existence. This is because it triggers the "fight-or-flight" response, which instructs you about when to respond in the face of adversity.

However, if this reaction is activated too frequently, it can harm psychological and physiological well-being. It has the potential to become deadly rather than useful. That's why it's critical to recognize and know your stress triggers before they create disruption.

- **Work Issues**

Workplace stress is among the most prominent sources of stress. Job stress is, in fact, more stressful than business, family obligations, or even individual health worries. Workers have to work long shifts for low remuneration during hard financial times. Uncertainty, ambiguity, and, of course, stress are all products of this atmosphere. Job stress refers to the negative reactions that arise when a job's demands do not meet the staff's talents, resources, or demands.

Job stress is not the same as the competition, which drives employees to develop and acquire new abilities. The difficulty is necessary for good work, and a little stress is OK. When stress frequently occurs, it can severely impact emotional well-being.

Factors That Cause Stress at Work

Both managers and workers can be affected by workplace stress. Although the economy is improving, job stability was a concern not long ago. Cutbacks, redundancies, acquisitions, and bankruptcy occur in various industries and organizations, resulting in significant changes for employees. Workers may experience additional responsibilities, high manufacturing demands, fewer perks, salary cutbacks, and more because they do not lose their jobs. This, in turn, produces a stressful climate in the workplace. Some of the factors that contribute to workplace stress are:

Managerial Style: It is another aspect in difficult work settings. Employees do not feel appreciated by their colleagues and bosses when there is inadequate interaction and workers are not engaged in judgment processes. Furthermore, a lack of relatives' regulations might result in greater stress due to work-life balance issues.

Professional Obligations: A major source of workplace stress is how duties are allocated and completed. Heavy workloads, occasional vacations, long shifts and transfers, superfluous regular activities, neglecting workers' skills, and other issues are examples.

Strategic Component Issues: It concerns job instability or a lack of promotion prospects, which are yet another source of workplace stress.

Catastrophic Occurrences: While not preferable, certain vocations are inherently riskier than some others. Every day, many lawyers and judges, firemen, first rescuers, and service members face challenging circumstances and put their lives in jeopardy. Ordinary tasks might become tough as a result of this. As a result, jobs like the ones described above are extremely stressful.

Working Conditions: While the majority of the preceding causes of work-related stress are psychological, poor working conditions can also produce stress on the body. Workplace stress may be caused by various factors, including loudness, loss of security, poor climate management, and insufficient amenities.

Workplace Stress Symptoms

Recognizing and learning about stress allows us to see how it may have a detrimental impact on the employees' health. Researchers have studied the link between occupational stress and health sickness for decades. Sleep difficulties, an upset stomach, and a headache are just a few examples of strained relationships with family members. Other signs and symptoms include:

- ✓ Lightheadedness
- ✓ Hypertensive
- ✓ Digestive problems
- ✓ Sleeping problems
- ✓ Mood swings
- ✓ Sadness
- ✓ Inability to pay attention
- ✓ Hunger loss
- ✓ Poor time management
- ✓ Ineffective work performance

- **Life Issues**

Several of the people we work with struggle with stress. We witness individuals feeling overworked due to the higher expectations and competition. So, what are among the most prevalent stress factors in modern society, and how can you combat them? Continue reading to learn more.

Interacting all the Time and Wanting to Accomplish Everything

We can communicate with individuals from all around the world, in multiple time zones, and gain an opportunity to get to know just by sitting idly behind our smartphones. Isn't it true that it makes us feel more connected? Of course, the solution isn't that straightforward. As technology advances, we're more likely to be hooked to our smartphones as business emails mount up. We're now continuously linked through social networks, which have positive and negative aspects.

Failure to Prioritize

Alongside attempting to accomplish too much, there is a lack of prioritization, resulting in the sense of being tugged in numerous ways in life without the need for a clear focus, aim, or goal. This can lead to a sense of unfulfilled potential, which, when combined with a workload, can cause emotional exhaustion.

Inappropriate Stress Release Mechanism

Stress is unavoidable in today's fast-paced world. Sadly, because most of us are short on time, our stress-relieving strategies are ineffective. However, if we are to battle stress, we must be on a strategic and tactical level in our fundamental building blocks. Otherwise, our health will confirm the stress we are experiencing.

Pollution

Poor air quality, noise, vibration, and visual intrusion are continual sources of stimulus wherever we go, it is not unexpected that we grow stressed due to being continuously linked to air pollution hurting our health and noise pollution harming our sense of hearing.

Self-Efficacy and Copying skills

People's inner views about their capacity to make an effect on factors that impact their lives are referred to as "self-efficacy." It is your conviction in your competence, both in terms of controlling your daily life and dealing successfully with specific activities. Self-efficacy explains your thoughts about your abilities to handle difficult events amid stress. A vast body of evidence suggests that having high levels of self-efficacy reduces people's chance of getting unpleasant emotional sensations by enhancing their feeling of control over the conditions they face.

The illusion of being in command buffers negative distress. People become anxious when they believe they are losing control, even though they are, in fact, in control and are unaware of it. Another reason people feel overwhelmed is that they feel lost since they lack the necessary coping abilities, resources, and capacity to deal effectively with the circumstance.

Coping Skills

A coping skill is a behavior or approach that aids in resolving a problem or fulfilling of demand. It is a problem-solving approach that makes it easier and quicker to address difficulties or fulfill demands than would otherwise be feasible.

Individuals who have learned a range of coping skills are better equipped to handle expectations and solve difficulties more readily and effectively than those who do not know how to interact. Persons with high coping skills are less prone to having psychological stress than individuals with less established coping skills, as they are more readily able to satisfy demands.

Learning how to cope is a talent that may be acquired. If you do not have adequate coping skills, you can learn strategies to improve your coping abilities over time. All stress-reduction tactics we will examine in this chapter can be considered coping skills. They are things that you may acquire and then "carry about" in your toolbox to assist you in improving your stress management skills.

Unrealistic Expectations

We all have aspirations for many aspects of our lives. As you get older, you gain them. Many of your assumptions are ones you aren't even aware of. Parents, authoritative figures, and other life experiences are frequently used as models.

Some aspirations are positive and can motivate you to face adversity and pursue your goals. However, when your aspirations are unreasonable, they can lead to conflict, miscommunication, dissatisfaction, and stress.

As a mature, you have the opportunity to examine your values and principles to determine whether you have ridiculous expectations. It's fine if you do. You can do actions to change your thinking and improve your life satisfaction. The trick is to become aware of your expectations and determine whether or not they are healthy. When your expectations are as follows, you know they're healthy:

- ✓ Courteous
- ✓ Reasonable
- ✓ Empathetic
- ✓ Considerate
- ✓ Sensible
- ✓ Truthful

If you have unreasonable expectations, though, you may put in a lot of work for little reward. Failing to accomplish an unachievable goal, such as becoming a billionaire by the age of 30, or having the "ideal" life or work, can lead to dissatisfaction, self-judgment, and even melancholy.

- **Change**

Even foreseen and anticipated lifestyle changes might be harder to modify than you think. Job changes and becoming a parent or quitting may have a significant impact on crucial aspects of your life, including:

- ✓ Wherever you reside
- ✓ How you describe yourself.
- ✓ Your life objectives
- ✓ The assumptions that others have of you
- ✓ Your convictions
- ✓ The people who are there to help you.

Negative emotions can be exacerbated by difficulties, obstacles, and conflicts with these life events. Please remember that a dramatic shift in one human's life might have a ripple effect throughout the family members. Having a baby, for example, involves more than only new duties and obligations for the parents. Everyone must make some adjustments as a result of these changes.

Change-related stress is an unavoidable aspect of life. Unfortunately, inadequate stress management may harm physical and psychological well-being. As a result, knowing how change causes stress and how to handle that stress is critical to living a healthy and happier life.

How Is Stress Caused by Change?

You will adapt to changes in a variety of ways throughout your life. Some of the changes are subtle and easily overlooked. Other changes might be more dramatic, resulting in increased stress. Transitions in one's life may be both pleasant and harmful.

- **Uncertainty**

Uncertainty makes it difficult for us to think ahead. Our minds typically make prospective choices regarding our past encounters. We can't count on past encounters to guide our judgment when the situation is unknown or we encounter something new. We might feel nervous about the coming if we don't have that tool, thinking through many situations and fretting about them.

Our mind loves to prepare for the future, utilizing our understanding of our previous experiences to predict what our future will contain. Fear of the unknown can cause psychological stress. It causes bodily changes such as hormone spikes and an elevated heart rate because it stimulates our fight-or-flight reaction. Chronic stress can negatively influence your health over time, raising your chance of heart disease and cognitive loss.

When doubt arises, people's negative ideas about uncertainty can contribute to detrimental emotional or behavioral reactions. Higher endurance for uncertainty might reduce stress levels by preventing individuals from obsessing over uncontrollable variables.

4.2 Effects on Your Life

There are various effects on our life. Some effects are on mental health, and some are on our physical health. Let's get into these.

- **Effects of Stress on Mental Health**

We will look at evidence of stress and mental health in this section.

Fight or flight is the Choice

The body undergoes physical changes as a result of stress. It raises the heart rate and respiration rate. The muscles stiffen up. The effectiveness of short-term memory improves. This stress has developed to protect people by preparing the body for a fight or flight reaction when we are in danger. According to research, cognitive skills enhance as stress levels rise. So, stress may be beneficial in little doses. It can assist us in preparing for a sporting event, a job interview, or an exam. The body usually recovers to its stable level following a stressful incident.

Long-term Anxiety

Various circumstances can trigger a stress reaction in the body. Organizational variables, sickness, disasters, marriage, family, financial, and housing issues can generate stress. Even apparently minor daily annoyances, such as someone pushing us in line, might cause us to become agitated. These scenarios have one thing in common: we can't foresee or control what's going on around us. Therefore, our bodies become more vigilant. And these occurrences might often occur, prompting the body's stress reaction repeatedly.

When the stressor is extended, it has a different effect than when used in brief bursts to help the body function better. The system that controls the stress reaction frequently cannot recover to its usual condition. Our ability to pay attention, remember things, and cope with feelings is harmed. Long-term stress can lead to physical and psychological disease through impacts on the heart, immunological and metabolic functioning, and chemicals acting on the brain.

Some of the behavioral and emotional signs of stress are similar to mental illnesses such as anxiety and melancholy. It can be difficult to tell where one starts and the other finishes, or which came first, due to this. A stressed person may feel anxious, depressed, able to fully focus or decide things, impatient, and furious.

The Science of Stress and Coping Strategies

Many people are more likely to experience depression and anxiety due to extreme stress. The specific processes that relate stress to mental illness are still being discovered.

Studies have revealed that the brain's first reaction to stress occurs within seconds of exposure to a stressor.' Neurotransmitters are produced. Stress hormones are then set to release, affecting areas of the brain that are important for cognition and emotion regulation. Cyclic stresses alter the ability of these systems to modulate the stress reaction.

Researchers are also looking at how these pathways are implicated in anxiety and depression, implying that stress and mental disease are linked biochemically. Prolonged stress has been demonstrated in studies to alter the development of the brain, particularly in regions that assist learning and memory. It can harm both nerve fibers and the connections that link them.

The Immunological System and Stress

The immune system is stimulated during the stress reaction, which helps to keep us secure. On the other hand, chronic stress and extended immune system activity may harm how the brain operates.

PTSD and Stress

Prolonged stress can sometimes lead to a mental disorder. After experiencing a traumatic or stressful incident, post-traumatic stress disorder (PTSD) can emerge. Someone whom the incident has impacted may have intense flashbacks or hallucinations and uncontrolled thoughts about it. Although certain risk factors are known, the precise cause of the illness is unknown.

- **Effects of Stress on Physical Health**

Even if you aren't aware of it, stress sensations may be hurting your health. You may believe that disease is responsible for that throbbing migraine, frequent sleeplessness, or a drop in work productivity. However, stress might be the root of the problem.

Stress symptoms can impact the body, your thoughts and emotions, and your actions. Recognizing typical stress symptoms might assist you in managing them. Unmanaged stress can lead to various health issues, including hypertension, cardiovascular disease, overweight, and diabetes. The following are physical signs of stress:

- Low energy consumption
- Brain fog
- Stomach issues
- Fatigue, pains, and tenseness
- Chest discomfort and a racing heart
- Sleeping problems
- Suffering from a lack of sexual arousal
- Anxiousness and trembling
- Difficulty swallowing
- Tightened Jaws and teeth chattering

The Impact of Workplace Stress

The fact of today's workplace is that stress is a fundamental and ubiquitous barrier to an organization and employee performance. Employees in a variety of industries and organizations must cope with stress. Bank employees are among those under a tremendous lot of stress due to a variety of stressors. Stress is linked to lower organizational performance, a high margin of error and poor reliability of job, turnover of employees, and absences due to health issues like anxiety, psychological disturbance, work-life stability, anxiety, and other diseases like frequent headaches and adiposity.

4.3 How to Manage Your Stress?

Most individuals encounter stress daily. Work, family troubles, health worries, and financial responsibilities are all factors that lead to increased stress levels. It's critical to recognize that stress is not the same as mental health illnesses like clinical depression, which require treatment. Although the suggestions below can help with a variety of stressors.

- **Take Care of Your Health**

Poor health habits can increase stress in your life and affect your ability to cope with it. Stress is a key result of bad health. Health issues have an impact on other aspects of your life. Health issues may make everyday chores more difficult, cause economic hardship, and even risk your ability to work. Taking care of the body will pay off in the long term. You must adopt these healthy practices to improve your life.

Consume a Balanced Diet

It is far more challenging to manage pressure and stress when you are famished or malnourished. Hunger may render you more cognitively receptive to events, causing you to get frustrated or enraged in reaction to little annoyances. Keeping a food diary may be a stress reducer as well as a healthcare saver.

Another advantage of eating healthy is that it may boost your mood. While the disadvantages of a bad diet build over a period and become increasingly apparent, a diet heavy in sweet, greasy, or nutritionally inadequate foods is considered least likely to make you feel good.

Prioritize Your Sleep

Sleep deprivation may significantly influence your general health and well-being in a negative way. Make a promise to yourself to get adequate sleep each night. You may be less efficient, less intellectually alert, and more susceptible to the impacts of stress if you haven't received enough sleep. Some helpful behaviors include:

- ✓ Each night, try to obtain a full 7 hours of sleep.
- ✓ After 2 p.m., avoid stimulants that have nicotine, such as tea and coffee.
- ✓ In the evening, stay away from meals that may cause you to lose sleep.
- ✓ Every night, go to bed at a decent hour; every morning, get up simultaneously.
- ✓ Create a calm resting environment by making sure that your bed is comfy and keeping the room at a normal temperature.
- ✓ Before going to bed, use a relaxing approach like mindfulness to calm you down.

- **Exercise Regularly**

Stretching your body regularly may make you feel less anxious. Taking aerobic activity twice a week substantially lowers your stress. In addition, the exercise practice decreases melancholy considerably. Several additional research has found that exercising lowers stress and improves mood, whereas an idle lifestyle can contribute to higher stress, bad mood, and sleep difficulties. Furthermore, daily exercise has been demonstrated to ease the symptoms of common mental health issues, including anxiety and sadness. Start with mild exercises like jogging or cycling. Picking an exercise that you like will increase your motivation to do exercise more.

- **Stop Using Nicotine Products**

Caffeine can upturn your nervous system and is present in espresso, tea, chocolates, and fizzy drinks. Anxiety can be exacerbated and increased by consuming too much caffeine in food. Furthermore, excessive drinking may disrupt your sleep. As a result, tension and anxiety problems may worsen.

The amount of caffeine that a person can tolerate varies from person to person. If caffeine causes you nervousness or anxiety, try switching to caffeine-free herbal tea or water instead of tea or caffeinated drinks.

Even though numerous studies demonstrate that coffee consumption is beneficial, but coffee consumption is advised to be kept under 380 mg per day, which equates to 4–5 cups of espresso. However, caffeine hypersensitive patients may suffer greater anxiety and tension after taking far less caffeine than this, so it's vital to think about your tolerance.

- **Practicing Relaxing Techniques**

Relaxation methods are an excellent strategy to handle stress. Tranquility isn't only about having a good time or doing something you love. Relaxation is a technique for reducing the adverse impact of stress on the brain and body. Relaxation techniques will help you deal with regular stress and strain connected to medical conditions such as cardiovascular disease and pain.

You can profit from mastering relaxation exercises whether your stress spirals out of control or you've successfully tamed it. It's simple to pick up some fundamental relaxation methods. Relaxation methods are also frequently free or inexpensive, involve no danger, and may be performed everywhere. Learn how to de-stress your life and improve your health by using these basic relaxation exercises.

Types of Relaxation Techniques

Health experts such as alternative healthcare personnel, physicians, and psychotherapists can teach different relaxation techniques. You may, however, practice some relaxing methods on your own if you like. Relaxation techniques, in general, entail redirecting your focus to something soothing and being more aware of your body. It makes no difference which meditation method you use. The important thing is that you make an effort to relax regularly to reap the advantages. The following are examples of relaxation techniques:

• Relaxation that is induced by the body. The term "autogenic" refers to anything that originates from within you. You combine both visuals and bodily awareness in this relaxing approach to alleviate tension. In your thoughts, you repeat words or ideas that may help you relax and relieve muscular tension. Imagine a tranquil scene and then concentrate on regulated, relaxing inhalation, decreasing your heart rate, or experiencing other sensations, such as resting each arm or leg one at a time.

• **Progressive Muscle Relaxation:** In this relaxation method, you focus on progressively tensing and then releasing each muscle group. This will assist you in focusing on the distinction between muscular tension and relaxation techniques. Physical sensations can be made more conscious.

Begin tensing and releasing the muscle in your toes and work your way up to your face and shoulders in one form of progressive muscle relaxation. Start with your head and neck and work your way down to your toes. Repeat by tensing your muscles for five seconds and then relaxing for 30 seconds.

• **Visualization:** With this relaxation technique, you may use mental pictures to take a mental trip to a tranquil, relaxing place or circumstance. When utilizing visualization to relax, attempt to include as many sensations as possible, such as smell, sight, sound, and touch. Consider the fragrance of salt water, the sound of waves crashing, and the sun's heat on your skin as you envision resting at the beach.

Close your eyes, find a quiet place to relax, and focus on your breathing. Concentrate on the present moment and imagine good ideas. It takes time to master relaxation methods. As you practice relaxation methods, you might become more conscious of muscular tightness and other physical stress feelings. You may make a concerted effort to practice a relaxation method the instant you begin to feel psychological stress if you understand how the stress reaction feels. This can help keep tension from getting out of hand.

Relaxation methods are skills, so keep that in mind. Your capacity to relax increases with practice, just like any other talent. Allow yourself to be tolerant. Allowing yourself to practice relaxation methods should not become a source of further stress.

Try a different relaxing method if one doesn't work for you. If none of your strain strategies seem to be working, speak to a doctor about additional possibilities.

Also, remember that certain people, particularly those with major psychiatric problems or a traumatic experience, may suffer emotional pain when using various relaxation techniques. Although it's uncommon if you feel emotional distress while using relaxation methods, stop and consult your psychologist or another mental health specialist.

Take Out Time for Your Self

Taking time for self-care might help you feel less stressed.

- Soaking in the tub
- Putting out candles
- Engrossing yourself in a good book
- Going to exercise
- Cooking a nutritious meal
- Relaxing before going to bed
- Relaxing with a massage

- Pursuing a pastime
- Utilizing calming smells in a diffuser
- Yoga practice

Self-care is linked to reduced stress levels and a greater quality of life. It is critical to set aside time for oneself to lead a healthy life. This is extremely critical for high-stress individuals, such as doctors, physicians, educators, and caregivers. Self-care doesn't seem to be difficult or time-consuming. It refers specifically to looking after your health and pleasure. Some smells, such as those found in candles or essential oils, can be particularly relaxing. Here are a few smells to help you relax:

- Lavender
- Rose
- Frankincense
- Sandalwood
- Geranium

Aromatherapy is the practice of using smells to improve one's mood. Aromatherapy has been shown in many trials to reduce stress and enhance relaxation.

Set Limits for Yourself and Learn to Say No

You don't have control over all stresses, but you have power over some of them. Taking on too much might increase your stress level and reduce the level of time you have for self-care. Taking charge of your own life can aid in stress reduction and mental health protection. Saying "no" more often might be one method to do this. This is particularly true if you discover yourself taking on even more obligations than you can manage since balancing many tasks might leave you exhausted.

Stress levels can be reduced by being cautious about what you take on — and expressing "no" to things that would needlessly add to your workload. Furthermore, setting boundaries — particularly with people who contribute to your stress levels — is a smart method to safeguard your wellness. This might be as easy as requesting a friend or relative not to drop by unexpectedly or canceling regular arrangements with a known person for causing problems.

Avoid Procrastination

Keeping on track of your goals and avoiding procrastination is another strategy to manage your stress. Procrastination can reduce your performance and force you to scramble to close the gap. This might lead to stress, which can negatively impact your health and sleep. If you notice yourself delaying frequently, it may be beneficial to develop the practice of establishing a prioritized to-do checklist. Set reasonable deadlines for yourself and work your way down on the list. Work on the tasks that need to be completed today and block off time for yourself.

Conclusion

The practice of identifying and expressing your feelings is known as emotional awareness. Emotional insight can help you better manage and maintain your mental health. When individuals experience a specific emotion, they usually have a bodily or mental reaction. You may determine when you encounter various emotions by paying enough attention to your own bodily and mental signs.

There are various steps you may take to assist you in managing your recognized emotions. As you've read before, many of them seem to be quite generic, but you should give them a shot since they could just work.

You can find a constructive outlet to communicate your feelings once you've learned to recognize their mental and bodily clues. Emotional expression is vital since repressing or denying emotions can result in negative consequences such as anger or stress. There are several methods to express your emotions productively and beneficially.

Anger is a strong emotion that can vary from minor annoyance to full-fledged anger. Although many people think of rage as just a "bad mood," it may also be beneficial. If allowed uncontrolled, anger can develop into violent action, such as screaming at someone or harming property. Angry sentiments might also force you to retreat from the public and focus your anger inside, which can negatively affect your health.

Managing your anger does not imply that you will never be furious. Rather, it entails learning to recognize, manage, and feel outraged healthily and constructively. Anger control is a skill that everyone can learn. There's always space for growth, even if you believe you've got your emotions under control.

Stress is an inescapable part of life. It is more crucial than ever to recognize stress and how to deal with it. While stress may be good, it can also be dangerous if prolonged. Once the body detects a crisis, it moves into constant alert mode, and it swiftly recovers after the threat has passed.

Health concerns, employment, income, family problems, discrimination or gender inequity, and everyday annoyances are all examples of stressors. Fortunately, there are some scientific proof treatments that can help you decrease stress and enhance your overall mental health.

Exercising, practicing meditation, enjoying hours with a pet, limiting screen time, and spending a lot of time outdoors are all beneficial strategies. It takes a lot of practice to become a good reactant. However, we can all improve our ability to cope with difficult emotions and express them in healthy ways. And it's something to rejoice over.

Printed in Great Britain
by Amazon

16898840R00047